THE A–Z OF WONDER WOMEN

YVONNE LIN

wren
&rook

CONTENTS

—

INTRODUCTION

This book is an illustrated alphabet of outstanding women.

The stories of their lives will inspire women everywhere, but particularly I hope that they will spark our kids as they grow up. My own little girl, Roni, is almost four years old now. Every day she doubts, tries, stumbles and achieves. She grows. Watching her, her friends and little girls on the street, I can't help but think about their future. Will they only dream, or will they succeed? What will keep them back? What can we do to help them reach their full potential?

Girls and boys need heroes as they grow up. They play with action figures, watch movies and read books. There are thousands upon thousands of books and movies about famous athletes, scientists, artists and explorers – but they're almost all men. Whatever a little boy wants to pursue, he sees the paths to success.

What role models does Roni have? Girls get princesses and mermaids – sure, not necessarily the worst career choices, but there are not enough castles and beaches for the world's 3.5 billion women.

And when women do excel in fields other than princess-ing and mermaid-ing, their accomplishments get pink-washed. Florence Nightingale becomes known as a sweet nurse who holds soldiers' hands through the night, rather than a statistician and analyst. Of all the Disney films, Roni loves *Mulan* best, a story about a girl who ran away from home, chopped off her hair, dressed as a man, joined the army, saved China from the invading Mongols, and became a war hero. But Mulan dolls only come with long flowing hair and a glittery ball gown.

Adults may not say these messages out loud, but kids see them day after day. Their futures and choices are introduced and reinforced again and again. It doesn't have to be this way. I created my book and populated it with twenty-six outstanding women from A to Z (and then some) to show kids how much women have achieved, even against overwhelming odds.

Roni and her friends will learn that little girls grew up and flew to the Moon; won the highest prizes in science and maths; led countries, armies, and even pirate fleets; became billionaires; and created Harry Potter.

I am more of an artist than I am a writer, so this book has more drawings than words. I hope readers will look at these women and imagine how they fought and succeeded. They are Aboriginal, Asian, African, white, young, old, strong, smart, harsh, kind, and stubborn. They show there is no *one* way to be a woman, or to succeed. And they make me proud.

I owe it to these women to bring them out of the shadows that history exiled them to. They will shine the light on the paths to success for our kids.

> 66
>
> THAT BRAIN OF MINE
> IS SOMETHING MORE
> THAN MERELY MORTAL,
> AS TIME WILL SHOW.
>
> 99

IS FOR ADA, ACE
OF ALGORITHMS

Ada Lovelace (1815–1852) was an English mathematician. She recognised the potential of the modern computer and wrote the first punch-card algorithm a century before the modern digital age. Ada was the first computer programmer.

> THOSE WHO DO ACHIEVE PEACE NEVER ACQUIESCE TO OBSTACLES, ESPECIALLY THOSE CONSTRUCTED OF BIGOTRY, INTOLERANCE AND INFLEXIBLE TRADITION.

B

IS FOR BENAZIR, BREAKER OF BOUNDARIES

Benazir Bhutto (1953–2007) was the first democratically elected female leader of a Muslim country. She served two terms as the prime minister of Pakistan, and was a champion of women's rights.

C

IS FOR CATHY, CHASER OF CHAMPIONSHIPS

Cathy Freeman (1973–) was the first female Aboriginal Commonwealth Games gold medal winner. After winning the 400 metres at the 2000 Summer Olympics, she took a victory lap carrying both the Aboriginal and Australian flags – despite the fact that unofficial national flags are banned at the Olympic Games.

—— 66 ——

THIS WAS MY RACE AND NO ONE WAS GOING TO STOP ME TELLING THE WORLD HOW PROUD I WAS TO BE ABORIGINAL.

—— 99 ——

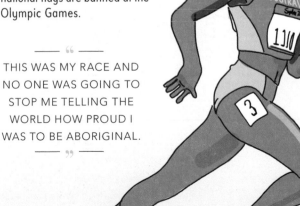

D

IS FOR DOROTHEA, DOCUMENTER OF THE DEPRESSION

Dorothea Lange (1895–1965) was an American photojournalist. Her iconic photographs exposed the plight of migrant workers and displaced farmers during the Great Depression in the 1930s. She showed the enormous power of documentary photography.

"
THE CAMERA IS AN INSTRUMENT
THAT TEACHES PEOPLE HOW TO
SEE WITHOUT A CAMERA.
"

$$\frac{\partial \psi}{\partial x^\mu} \psi \big) \eta^{\nu\mu}$$

E

IS FOR EMMY, ENCHANTER OF EQUATIONS

> " MY METHODS [OF ALGEBRA] ARE REALLY METHODS OF WORKING AND THINKING; THIS IS WHY THEY HAVE CREPT IN EVERYWHERE, ANONYMOUSLY. "

Emmy Noether (1882–1935) was a German-American mathematician. Einstein called her 'the most significant creative mathematical genius thus far produced since the higher education of women began.' Emmy devised Noether's theorem, which paved the way for advances in many areas of physics.

IS FOR FLORENCE, FIGHTER OF FILTH

Florence Nightingale (1820–1910) was an English statistician and the founder of modern nursing. Her statistics work has saved countless lives. She discovered that poor sanitary conditions were the main cause of death in hospitals, and encouraged new practices, such as hand-washing, to combat this.

DIAGRAM OF THE CAUSES OF MORTALITY
IN THE ARMY IN THE EAST.

APRIL 1854 · MAY · JUNE · JULY · AUGUST · SEPTEMBER · OCTOBER · NOVEMBER · DECEMBER

" HOW VERY LITTLE CAN
BE DONE UNDER THE
SPIRIT OF FEAR. "

G

IS FOR GRACE, GUTSY GAL OF THE GALLEON

Grace O'Malley (1530–1603) was an ambitious Irish pirate queen. Grace and her crew dominated the coast of Ireland by raiding merchant ships, conquering castles from rival clans and battling English armies.

> "
> SHE HAD STRONGHOLDS
> ON HER HEADLANDS,
> AND BRAVE GALLEYS
> ON THE SEA,
> AND NO WARLIKE
> CHIEF OR VIKING,
> E'ER HAD BOLDER
> HEART THAN SHE.
> "
>
> FROM THE SONG
> *GRANUAILE*

H

IS FOR HARRIET, HIKER OF THE HIGHLANDS

> " I'VE NEVER FOUND MY SEX A HINDERMENT; NEVER FACED A DIFFICULTY, WHICH A WOMAN, AS WELL AS A MAN, COULD NOT SURMOUNT. "

Harriet Chalmers Adams (1875–1937) was an American explorer, writer and photographer. She travelled more than 160,000 kilometres, discovering Incan ruins, canoeing the Amazon and traversing the Andes. She shared her stories in *National Geographic* magazine, and was one of the most popular adventure lecturers of her time.

> "
> I WAS BROUGHT UP TO
> BELIEVE THAT A PERSON
> MUST BE RESCUED WHEN
> DROWNING, REGARDLESS OF
> RELIGION AND NATIONALITY.
> "

I

IS FOR IRENA, INTREPID SAVIOUR OF INFANTS

Irena Sendler (1910–2008) was a Polish nurse and humanitarian. Irena and her co-workers smuggled approximately 2,500 Jewish children out of the Warsaw Ghetto. They provided the children with false identity papers and shelter. Irena saved more Jews than any other individual during the Holocaust.

J

IS FOR J.K., JUVENILE JOY BRINGER

J. K. Rowling (1965–) is a British writer. Despite first being rejected by 12 publishers, *Harry Potter and the Philosopher's Stone* started a literary revolution. Millions of formerly reluctant young readers have eagerly read all 3,407 pages of her Harry Potter books.

IT MATTERS NOT
WHAT SOMEONE IS
BORN, BUT WHAT
THEY GROW TO BE.

K

IS FOR KATE,
KEEN CAPTAIN
OF WOMANKIND

Kate Sheppard (1847–1934) was the leader of the New Zealand suffragists. She wrote pamphlets, edited the first woman-operated newspaper, and helped gather 30,000 signatures in a petition that was presented to Parliament. As a result, in 1893, New Zealand became the first country to give women the right to vote.

WE ARE TIRED OF HAVING A 'SPHERE' DOLED OUT TO US, AND OF BEING TOLD THAT ANYTHING OUTSIDE THAT SPHERE IS 'UNWOMANLY'.

L

IS FOR LYDA, LEADER OF THE LAW

Lyda Conley (1869–1946) was a Wyandot-American lawyer. She was the first Native American woman to bring a case before the US Supreme Court. Lyda was the first person to argue that Native American burial grounds are entitled to protection from the US Government.

> "
> IN THIS CEMETERY ARE BURIED ONE-HUNDRED OF OUR ANCESTORS...WHY SHOULD WE NOT BE PROUD OF OUR ANCESTORS AND PROTECT THEIR GRAVES?
> "

M

IS FOR MARIA,
MASTER OF
MONTESSORI

Maria Montessori (1870–1952) was one of Italy's first female physicians and a trailblazing education innovator. Maria designed learning materials and a classroom environment that builds on the way children naturally learn, and she opened the first Montessori school.

—— " ——

THIS IS OUR MISSION:
TO CAST A RAY OF LIGHT
AND PASS ON.

—— " ——

N

IS FOR NELLIE, NERVY NARRATOR OF THE NAKED TRUTH

Nellie Bly (1864–1922) was an American investigative journalist and adventurer. She went undercover to expose the conditions of asylum patients on Blackwell's Island, New York. Nellie's work changed public policy, her outfits influenced fashion trends and her adventures inspired board games.

> I TOOK IT UPON MYSELF TO ENACT THE PART OF A POOR, UNFORTUNATE, CRAZY GIRL, AND FELT IT MY DUTY TO NOT SHIRK ANY OF THE DISAGREEABLE RESULTS THAT SHOULD FOLLOW.

—— 66 ——

KNOW WHAT SPARKS THE
LIGHT IN YOU. THEN USE THAT
LIGHT TO ILLUMINATE THE WORLD.

—— 99 ——

IS FOR OPRAH, OPEN-HEARTED ORATORY POWERHOUSE

Oprah Winfrey (1954–) is an American media mogul. She was born into a poor family in rural Mississippi. From her humble beginnings, she worked her way up to become North America's first African-American multibillionaire and one of the most influential women of her generation.

P

IS FOR PATSY, PREJUDICE-OPPOSED POLITICIAN

Patsy T. Mink (1927–2002) was an American politician who fought gender and racial discrimination. She was the first non-white woman elected to the US Congress. She co-wrote, sponsored and secured the passage of Title IX, which prohibited gender discrimination by government-funded institutions.

> IT IS EASY ENOUGH TO VOTE RIGHT AND BE CONSISTENTLY WITH THE MAJORITY. BUT IT IS MORE IMPORTANT TO BE AHEAD OF THE MAJORITY AND THIS MEANS BEING WILLING TO CUT THE FIRST FURROW IN THE GROUND AND STAND ALONE FOR A WHILE IF NECESSARY.

TITLE IX

IS FOR QIU, QUICK-FOOTED AND QUOTABLE FEMINIST FIGHTER

Qiu Jin (1875–1907) was a Chinese revolutionary, feminist and writer. She founded a newspaper in which she spoke out for women's rights, including freedom from oppressive marriages, education and the abolishment of foot binding. And she was a martial artist, who trained an army of female revolutionaries.

"
DON'T TELL ME WOMEN ARE NOT THE STUFF OF HEROES.
"

> WHEN I'M SOMETIMES
> ASKED WHEN WILL THERE
> BE ENOUGH [WOMEN ON
> THE SUPREME COURT]
> AND I SAY WHEN THERE
> ARE NINE, PEOPLE ARE
> SHOCKED. BUT THERE'D
> BEEN NINE MEN, AND
> NOBODY'S EVER RAISED A
> QUESTION ABOUT THAT.

R

IS FOR RUTH, ROBED IN REASON

Ruth Bader Ginsburg (1933–) is the second female US Supreme Court Justice. She is an advocate for the advancement of gender equality and women's rights. Before becoming a judge, Ruth co-founded the Women's Rights Project at the American Civil Liberties Union and argued six gender discrimination cases before the Supreme Court, winning five.

> I AM A WOMAN WHO CAME FROM THE COTTON FIELDS OF THE SOUTH. I WAS PROMOTED FROM THERE TO THE WASHTUB. THEN I WAS PROMOTED TO THE COOK KITCHEN. AND FROM THERE I PROMOTED MYSELF INTO THE BUSINESS OF MANUFACTURING HAIR GOODS AND PREPARATIONS...I HAVE BUILT MY OWN FACTORY ON MY OWN GROUND.

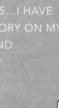

S

IS FOR SARAH, SELF-MADE MILLIONAIRE OF STUNNING HAIR

Sarah Breedlove (1867–1919) was the first female American self-made millionaire. She made her fortune by developing and marketing a line of beauty and hair products for black women. She also showed women how to budget and build their own businesses, and encouraged them to become financially independent.

T

IS FOR TINA, TITILLATING TICKLER

Tina Fey (1970–) is an American comedian and producer. She became hit TV show *Saturday Night Live*'s first female head writer. Since then, she has written and starred in films and TV shows including *Mean Girls* and *30 Rock*.

> 66
>
> YOU CAN'T BE THAT KID STANDING AT THE TOP OF THE WATER SLIDE, OVERTHINKING IT. YOU HAVE TO GO DOWN THE CHUTE.
>
> 99

U

IS FOR URSULA, UNBOUND AUTHOR OF UNCOMMON WORLDS

Ursula K. Le Guin (1929–2018) was an American writer. She won every major science-fiction award possible, most more than once. Ursula's fully imagined worlds challenge readers to question conventions of gender, race, the environment and society.

V

IS FOR VALENTINA, VANGUARD SPACE VOYAGER

Valentina Tereshkova (1937–) is a Russian cosmonaut and an engineer. As a young woman, she skydived as a hobby, and in 1963 she became the first woman in space. She orbited Earth 48 times. In 2013, she offered to go on a one-way trip to Mars.

ON EARTH, MEN AND WOMEN
ARE TAKING THE SAME RISKS.
WHY SHOULDN'T WE BE TAKING
THE SAME RISKS IN SPACE?

W

IS FOR WAJEHA, WISE WARRIOR FOR WOMEN

Wajeha al-Huwaider (1962–) is a Saudi activist. She campaigns against laws that give men control over women. In 2008, she filmed herself driving, which was illegal for women in Saudia Arabia at that time, and posted it on YouTube. In 2013, she was sentenced to 10 months in prison for attempting to help a woman escape her abusive husband.

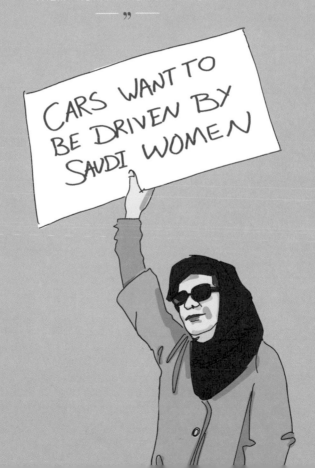

X

IS FOR XUE, XENACIOUS EXPLORER OF THE UNHEARD

Xue Xinran (1958–) is a Chinese-British journalist. She shocked China when she broke taboos and created a radio show to tell the heartbreaking and never-before-heard women's stories of forced marriages, child abuse, foot binding and oppression.

— 66 —

I DISCOVERED THAT WOMEN HAD NO IDEA HOW TO TALK ABOUT THEMSELVES.

— 99 —

Y

IS FOR YAYOI, YARDS OF YUMMY DOTS

Yayoi Kusama (1929–) is an eccentric Japanese artist. Her work has influenced Keith Haring, David Hockney and Andy Warhol. Yayoi creates sculptures, paintings and dizzying and dazzling polka-dot-filled walk-in installations.

" EVERY TIME I HAVE HAD A PROBLEM, I HAVE CONFRONTED IT WITH THE AXE OF ART. "

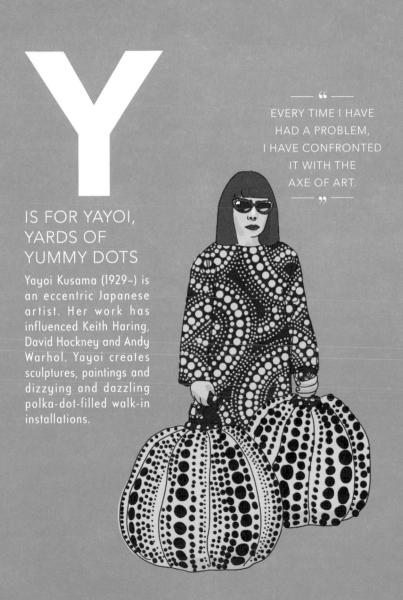

Z

IS FOR ZAHA, ZESTFULLY ZANY ARCHITECT

Zaha Hadid (1950–2016) was an Iraqi-British architect. Known as the 'Queen of the Curve', she created breathtakingly expressive buildings. She was the first woman to receive the prestigious Pritzker Architecture Prize.

— " —
I DON'T THINK
THAT ARCHITECTURE IS
ONLY ABOUT SHELTER...
IT SHOULD BE ABLE TO
EXCITE YOU, TO CALM YOU,
TO MAKE YOU THINK.
— " —

30

MORE WONDER WOMEN

Selecting just 26 wonder women to include in this book was a difficult task – so I'm making room for 30 more here. These women redefined gender, fought poverty, climbed mountains, saved lives and more. They are inspiring, amazing and awesome.

ANGELA MERKEL (1954–) is one of the most powerful women in the world. She has been the Chancellor of Germany since 2005 and often acts as the leader of the European Union.

BILLIE JEAN KING (1943–) was the top-ranked female tennis player in the world in 1967, and one of the first openly gay athletes. Billie fought for equal prize money for female tennis players.

BOUDICCA (30–61) was a Celtic warrior queen who led a rebellion in Britain against the occupying Roman Empire. Boudicca's warriors obliterated the Roman Ninth Legion.

CHIEN-SHIUNG WU (1912–1997) was a nuclear physicist. Chien was a Princeton University faculty member before women were admitted, and she designed an experiment known as the "Wu experiment" for which her colleagues were awarded the Nobel Prize.

CHIMAMANDA NGOZI ADICHIE (1977–) is a feminist poet and novelist who won a MacArthur Genius Grant. Her essay *We Should All Be Feminists* is witty, personal and compelling.

CHING SHIH (1775–1844) was the most successful pirate of all time. She controlled the China Sea with a fleet of around 1,500 ships and 80,000 sailors, and created a strict code of pirate law with special protections for female captives.

ELLEN DEGENERES (1958–) risked her career when she came out as gay in 1997. Her sitcom *Ellen* was cancelled and she couldn't get a job for years. Ellen "kept on swimming" though, and went on to create the stunningly successful *The Ellen DeGeneres Show*.

EMMELINE PANKHURST (1858–1928) was a leader of the British suffragettes. She founded the Women's Social and Political Union and fought for the right to vote. She was often imprisoned for detaining politicians and organising rallies.

GERTRUDE BELLE ELION (1918–1999) was a biochemist who won the Nobel Prize in Physiology or Medicine for research that would lead to the creation of AZT, the drug that prevents and treats HIV and AIDS. She also developed anti-rejection medications that are used to treat organ transplant patients.

GRACE MURRAY HOPPER (1906–1992) was a mathematician, Navy admiral and computer programming pioneer. She led the team that created the first computer language compiler.

HARRIET TUBMAN (1822–1913) escaped slavery in the US, then made 19 trips to the South and led around 70 slaves to freedom in the North. After the Civil War ended, Harriet devoted her life to helping former slaves.

JACINDA ARDERN (1980–) is Prime Minister of New Zealand. She was elected at 37, making her the world's youngest female head of government. She has reached out to the underserved indigenous Maori communities.

JANE GOODALL (1934–) is the world's leading expert on chimpanzees. Jane spent 55 years studying and living with wild chimpanzees in Tanzania and now advocates for ecological conservation and animal welfare.

JEANNE BARÉT (1740–1807) was the first woman to travel around the world. Since women were not permitted on official expedition ships, she disguised herself as a man and enlisted as a valet.

JULIA GILLARD (1961–) was the first (and so far only) female prime minister of Australia. She led the country between 2010–2013, and now is launching the Global Institute for Women's Leadership, to get more women around the world into leadership roles.

LHAKPA SHERPA (1973–) holds the world record for summits of Everest by a woman – by the time she was 45, she had climbed the mountain 8 times! Lhakpa also works as a dishwasher at Whole Foods in Connecticut, USA, so that her daughters can go to the best schools.

LISE MEITNER (1878–1968) was a nuclear physicist who led a group of scientists who discovered fission. She should have been awarded the Nobel Prize for the discovery, as her collaborator Otto Hahn was.

MAE JEMISON (1956–) entered Stanford University at 16. After graduating, she went to Cornell Medical College and worked as a Peace Corp doctor in Sierra Leone and Liberia. She went on to become the first African-American female astronaut.

MALALA YOUSAFZAI (1997–) is a girls' education activist and the youngest ever Nobel Prize winner. Aged eleven, she started writing a blog advocating for girls' education in Pakistan under Taliban rule. Aged fifteen, she was shot by the Taliban in retaliation.

MARY SHELLEY (1797–1851) wrote *Frankenstein* and several other novels. With *Frankenstein*, Mary may have invented the genre of science fiction. She was the daughter of radical feminist Mary Wollstonecraft.

MARY WOLLSTONECRAFT (1759–1797) was one of the first feminist philosophers. In *A Vindication of the Rights of Woman*, she writes that women should not be treated like ornaments or property and that they deserve the same rights as men.

MARYAM MIRZAKHANI (1977–2017) was the first woman to win the Fields Medal, the most prestigious mathematics award in the world. As a teenager, she and her friend Roya Beheshti were the first two girls on Iran's Mathematical Olympiad team.

MISTY COPELAND (1982–) is the first African-American woman to be a principal dancer in the American Ballet Theater, one of the leading classical ballet companies in the United States.

NANCY WAKE (1912–2011) was a French spy during the Second World War. In 1943, Wake was at the top of the Gestapo's most wanted list, with a 5,000,000 franc price on her head.

NESS KNIGHT (1985–) is a South African endurance adventurer. Ness ran 15 marathons in 15 days, crossed the Namib Desert alone, swam the River Thames from its source to London, and cycled across Bolivia with no money.

NOOR INAYAT KHAN (1914–1944) was Britain's first Muslim war heroine, and the first female radio operator secret agent – an incredibly dangerous job. The average life span for the job was six weeks, and Noor lasted almost four months.

RESHMA SAUJANI (1975–) is the founder of Girls Who Code, a nonprofit organisation that has helped more than 90,000 girls in the US learn how to code. Reshma's TED talk is, "Teach girls bravery, not perfection."

TOMOE GOZEN (12th century) was a samurai warrior. It was written that, "so dexterously did she handle sword and bow that she was a match for a thousand warriors."

VIGDÍS FINNBOGADÓTTIR (1930–) was the first woman in the world to be elected president in a democratic election. She was elected president of Iceland in 1980 and reelected three times after that. She fought for parental leave, and to close the gender pay gap.

WANG ZHENYI (1768–1797) was a Chinese scientist and mathematician at a time when almost no women were educated. She wrote at least 12 books on subjects such as the Pythagorean Theorem, trigonometry and solar eclipses.

WANGARI MAATHAI (1940–2011) founded the Green Belt Movement which works with rural Kenyan women to plant trees to protect the soil, store rainwater and provide food and firewood. In 2004, she won the Nobel Peace Prize.